DevOps Handbook

A Guide to Implementing DevOps In Your Workplace

WorldTech

© 2017

The information provided herein is stated to be truthful and consistent, in that any liability, in terms of inattention or otherwise, by any usage or abuse of any policies, processes, or directions contained within is the solitary and utter responsibility of the recipient reader. Under no circumstances will any legal responsibility or blame be held against the publisher for any reparation, damages, or monetary loss due to the information herein, either directly or indirectly.

Respective authors own all copyrights not held by the publisher.

The information herein is offered for informational purposes solely, and is universal as so. The presentation of the information is without contract or any type of guarantee assurance.

The trademarks that are used are without any consent, and the publication of the trademark is without permission or backing by the trademark owner. All trademarks and brands within this book are for clarifying purposes only and are the owned by the owners themselves, not affiliated with this document.

Table of Contents

Introduction

If you have landed on this page, then chances are, your company needs a little push in order to work effectively. If you are still stuck in the 90s when it comes to methods of operating, tools, and processes, then buying this book is the best chance for you to join the modern agile era.

DevOps is not just a buzzword. It is a mindset that can pull your companies problems by the root and change the traditional, core beliefs. When the old waterfall methods cannot provide you with the desired outcome, it is time for a total transformation that can get you off the downward spiral.

Teaching you the ultimate ways to start implementing DevOps in order to decrease the deployment time and maximize the profit, this book will show you why some of the world's largest companies have chosen to think DevOps.

Click the 'buy' button to reveal how to take advantage of this new methodology.

The Importance of DevOps

What is the one thing that every business needs? Communication and collaboration. And while the fact that the two hair dressers don't speak to each other may not mean the end for that small hair salon, poor working collaboration can force larger companies to shut their doors.

And since you are reading this book, I am pretty sure you can relate to this destructive working pattern. Almost every company is working under circumstances that are far from ideal. Systems break down, shipments get delayed, service becomes unsatisfactory. Does it ring a bell? Unfortunately, we are all familiar with this vicious cycle because that is the world we live in.

Now, imagine this from a more specific perspective. Imagine what this core conflict may mean for companies that have goals that depend upon IT and Development Operations. In fact, let's imagine a similar scenario.

Almost every problem that happens within these companies is divided in two parts. The first part of the problem starts with the IT department when there is a fragile application that can cause an outrageous impact (not a positive one!) for the company. And the worst part is not in the fact that the application is fragile, but in the way we find out about its delicate condition. Instead of having regular monitoring and testing that can alarm us that there might be a potential problem, we'd rather 'feel' it instead. Usually it is the salesperson letting us know that some of our profit-making pipelines has stopped working.

What does that mean? That means that we have just encountered a situation, a problem that we weren't planning for and don't know how to solve. That means that we need to spend more time and energy trying to find the solution on the expense of our already scheduled work actions. That means that we have to put our usual work 'on hold', so we can fix the problem and become able to continue with our work.

But that is not the worst part. The worst part is the second part of our problem, which is about to happen.

The second part of the problem happens in the Development department. Once we find ourselves unable to provide the usual services due to the unexpected problem, we begin to let people down. We find ourselves unable to achieve what we have promised to our customers, analysts, or investors, and that's when the real problem arises. We start lying. We fall into an even deeper abyss, all in attempt to pick ourselves up from down there. We make even bigger promises, lying both ourselves and the customers.

This chronic conflict forces us to encounter more and more urgent projects placed behind the waiting line, which leaves us no other choice but to cut corners. Once the security, management, and other not-that-functional corners are being cut, technical debt slowly comes our way. And technical, just like any other debt, begins to pile up, until we face an even bigger financial problem. That results in late deployments. Things that shouldn't require more than a few hours now take days to complete. The struggle to deploy on time basically causes anarchy.

This unhealthy working environment forces the Dev and Ops guys to work super hard to try to fix the problem, and to find the answer to what it seems to be a never-ending quarrel over who started the problem. Was it the IT department whose application broke down, or are the Development people to blame for making promises that they were unable to achieve?

I am sure that many can relate to this imaginary scenario, since most of the companies work that way. But is there anything that can pull the companies out of this downward spiral? Meet DevOps, the knight in shiny armor for most companies.

DevOps offers the ideal solution to the previous scenario. It is what breaks the conflict and makes both departments to communicate, collaborate, and work together toward solving the problem without disrupting product making or service providing. It is the fastest and best way to reduce the time for deployments in order for the companies to quickly seize market opportunities and receive customer feedback fast.

For those of you who think that it is impossible for the both sides to get along so well and find a common goal, just think about what Facebook or Amazon does. Do you think that without DevOps they would have been able to provide their services the way they do? I highly doubt it. These huuuge companies have thousands of deployments per day, and without a middle ground such as DevOps, they would never be able to be as successful.

If you have chosen this book to learn where and how to start introducing DevOps to your company, then you are in luck. These next few chapters will tell you everything you need to know about this new and amazing approach.

DevOps and the Other Guys (Agile and Continuous Delivery)

When the term Agile Development was first introduced to the world in 2001, it caused some serious changes in the modern software development. Since then, the software development has noticeably changed its course, shifting from the waterfall models (although this traditional approach is still known to have loyal supporters) to a leaner and agiler methodology.

The agile methodology gives companies the ability to become quickly responsive to unpredictability through work that is both iterative and incremental. The initial goal of the Agile Manifesto creators was to make a set of values and principles that would help companies to deliver working software quickly and frequently. You can say that its main aim is increasing the productivity of the development organizations.

DevOps vs Continuous Delivery

But the technology progresses as the time goes by. Many things have changed since Agile became a thing. When the demand for service development began to reach for the skies, some of the leading 'thinkers' in the software world have managed to come up with even more specific terms than Agile. That's how DevOps and Continuous Delivery were born.

But even though these two seem to be children of Agile, they are more different than you may think. The distinction may be a little fogy, and these two are often used interchangeably, but the truth is, DevOps and Continuous Delivery do not represent the same. Why is this important to know? If your company craves DevOps skills and you are looking for a way to implement its strategies, knowing this distinction is not only beneficial, but crucial.

So, what exactly is the difference between these two? There may be some common traits that are shared by these methodologies, such as being agile-aimed, relying on collaborating with the IT department, and faster service marketing, but their main focus is still different.

DevOps is focused on aligning the development and operations department and merging the processes that these two roles manage.

Continuous Delivery is mainly focused on making reliable releases in order to deliver frequently and on time, and receive fast feedback.

Although this may confuse you even more and make you picture them as two main parts of a whole, DevOps being the machine and CD being the conveyer belt that transfers the products, the difference is greater than that. DevOps is more about the culture and is the strong link that connects two different departments into working together towards achieving business goals.

Getting Started with DevOps

You may be a step away from introducing DevOps to your company, but there are quite a few things you need to know and determine, in order to start the DevOps journey the right way and make sure that you are not about to make a quick decision that might backfire.

From selecting the right value stream to designing your organization with the Conway's law, this chapter will teach you everything you have to know before starting with DevOps.

The Value Stream

Can you delay the service and not deliver to the customers? Of course you can. But, can you really afford it? When holding features and not releasing them to the customer in time, there are more than one way in which you are hurting your company. The first one of all is the holding cost, then there is the opportunity cost, cost of uncertainty, cost of delay... Should I go on? It think we all got the picture, the greater the costs, the quicker you would want to deliver your services. That is why it is in every company's best interest to deliver small batches of features frequently, instead of delivering big batches once a week or once a month. This is not only in the best interest in terms of the costs, but also convenience. If a certain product somehow gets misplaced or undelivered, it does not have to wait for the BIG batch, but it can be quickly shipped with the next release train.

But in order to reduce the size of the batch and increase the frequency of deployment, it will take us a lot more than what we used to spend before. That is why looking at the whole picture of value stream that will allow us to turn our concept into cash, is crucial.

Why do you think not all companies have implanted DevOps? Because not everyone can afford it. Reducing the deployment time, as well as the cost for transport require some serious investment. You need to invest in techniques, tools, and most importantly, leadership. Adopting DevOps may seem like a simple thing, but we are talking about adopting a culture after all. A mindset that has to be accepted by all the employees. DevOps is not something that you can simply purchase. It is a way of software-development thinking that has to be adopted by both the IT and Development departments.

However, do not let this discourage you. If you don't think that you can pull it off by yourself, know that you can hire a DevOps consultant or maybe a Lean-Agile coach who will pinpoint which areas are worth investing in.

What to Start with?

Selecting which value stream to start with is a process that needs to be carefully thought through, since the value stream will not only be in charge of the transformation of your business, but it will also decide who should be transformed.

When choosing a value stream, there are three main aspects that you need to pay special attention to:

Greenfield or Brownfield?

If you have done some urban planning, chances are you have come across these terms before. Greenfield developments is a term used to describe those buildings that are built on undeveloped land, while brownfield developments is used for buildings on a land that someone used for industrial purposes.

In technology, these terms are used similarly. Greenfield development means making a project from scratch or building an application anew. Brownfield projects, on the other hand, are used to describe those applications that are in service and have been offering their service to customers for some time. Just like the brownfield buildings, the application of this kind are also 'polluted'. Not with some hazardous waste, but with technical debt.

And while greenfield projects are safer and easier to build, DevOps has a history of successfully transforming different types of brownfield projects. In fact, the famous eCommerce platform Etsy used to be a brownfield project.

Systems of Records and Systems of Engagement
Recently, Gartner Research has introduced a new framework within the IT world. According to them, those enterprises that offer wide services can no longer benefit from the traditional practices of development. Therefore, they popularized the bimodal IT framework

that consists of two parallel tracks. One of them support fast development of innovative applications, while the other one is in charge of maintaining and operating existing projects.

Within this bimodal IT strategy, there are two systems found:

Systems of Record – According to Gartner, these systems are in charge of 'doing things right'. They are literally the spine of enterprises, they have regulatory requirements, and are not prone to change.

Systems of Engagement – Unlike the systems of record, these systems change rapidly, are focused on supporting fast feedback loops, and are mostly focused on 'doing things fast'.

Expanding the Concept

Like I said, DevOps is a mindset. A belief and idea that not everyone in the company is willing to share with you. And that is okay. Everyone is entitled to have an opinion. Once the concept is presented in the company, there will be group division. Some will have more conservative attitude, while others will be thrilled of the new ideas.

The point is not to waste your time or energy trying to 'convert' the conservative ones into accepting the new methodology, but try to work as much as you can with the early adopters. That should be your starting off point. From there, you are supposed to build your base. There are three main steps to expanding the concept of DevOps through your organization:

- *Finding the Early Adopters*. Your main job in the beginning is to find those who are supportive of the new work concept. The ideal scenario would be if these were highly respected people with a huge influence over the other people in the company. But, even if that is not the case, that does not mean that your DevOps journey is doomed to fail.

- *Working with the Supporters.* In this phase you have to expand your DevOps ideas to more teams in order to create your base of people who support you. Even if these people are not the most influential folks in the company, you need to put your focus into expending the coalition you have with the supporters in order to bring more success to the company. It is really important to be able to show the others some early wins. In order to do so, it is suggested that you break up the larger successes into smaller steps. This is also good for detecting your mistakes early.

- *Identifying the Great Dictators.* In most cases, there is some high-profile, influential person who is against the idea of bringing transformation with DevOps. These people will most likely resist your every effort to apply those changes. Do not waste your energy with this group before you can actually demonstrate some success because you will probably lose the battle. Try to talk with the 'dictators' only when you find strong arguments.

Mapping

After you find which value stream you want to apply your DevOps to, your very next step should be to determine exactly how your company delivers this value to your customers. You need to find out who performs what work, and what you can do in order to boost the productivity even more.

To do so, you should create a list of all of your value stream members who work together, from product owners and development, all the way to the technology executives and managers.

After you are familiar with the value stream members and how they contribute to service delivery, the next step is to create a map that will show exactly how the work is performed. Creating a value stream map can really make all the difference, especially in these early stages of adopting the DevOps culture.
This very important step will help you:

-   Provide context to your technical experts who examine the technology.

- Provide a great baseline for you to easily measure the improvements that have been made after adopting DevOps.

- Start to win both hearts and minds. By working together, the Dev and Ops will gain a good understanding of how their work helps the company move uphill or downhill.

So, how to build this map? Your map should show clear steps where all the improvements can be easily spotted. You don't need to create a complex spaghetti diagram in order to record the work it takes your value stream team to deliver service to customers. All you need to do is create a simple diagram with no more than 10-15 process blocks. These blocks must include the lead time it takes a process to be finished, as well as the value added time.

Designing with Conway's Law

The old Conway's law can be very successfully implemented on your value stream. The Conway's Law says that the way in which we organize our team will not only have a huge impact on the software we develop, but also on the outcome of our production.

If you want the Operations department to receive a very fast work flow from the people in Development, then organizing your team with the help of the Conway's law is your best strategy.

To do so, you need to *evaluate the archetypes of the organization*. There are three types of structures that you could use to organize your team with the Conway's law:

1. *Functional* – The organizations that are functional-oriented are in charge of unifying the skills, which supports career growth. They have a hierarchical structure. This has been the main method of organizing Operations (database admins, server admins, etc.)

2. _Market_ – Those organizations that are market-oriented are focused on quickly answering to customers. They usually include cross-functional disciplines, and are centered on the customer's needs. This is how most of the companies that have adopted DevOps work (for instance Amazon, Etsy, Netflix, etc.)

3. _Matrix_ – The matrix organizations are a combination of the functional and market organizations. Although they are generally in charge of observing, it is a common occurrence for those who are a part of these organizations to have to respond to more than two managers.

Although traditional IT departments use the functional organizations, that is not ideal, especially not if you have adopted DevOps. In order to achieve the desired DevOps result, you need to lower the impact of functional orientations and shift towards speed optimizing, which market orientation is all about.

However, you need to be careful as to how you plan on achieving the market orientation. If you choose to make a giant top-to-bottom reorganization, that will most likely backfire, as it can create fear amongst the people in your company and result in work disruption. Instead of doing that, you need to implant the functional skills into every service team, for instance Infosec or Ops. This can enable the team to deliver the service directly to the customer without having to actually work with the guys in Ops or Infosec.

Developing the Habits

After evaluating the organizational archetypes, it is time to develop these habits in the people from your value stream team.

Knowing the Priorities

What should be everyone's job is making sure that the customers are satisfied. That means that testing, operating, and ensuring security, must be a priority of every person from the value stream tea, regardless of the type of work they do.

Deploying the work to customers must be the most urgent problem, every single day.

Make Everyone a Generalist

When I say allowing everyone to be a generalist, I mean rotating people through a number of different roles. Just because someone is in charge of running a system, doesn't mean that they shouldn't know how the system is actually built. The term 'full stack engineer' is now widely used to describe those people who are not only generalist, but also have a decent knowledge of the entire stack of the process, whether it is database, networking, or application code.

It is very important for people who are adopting DevOps, to also adopt the growth mindset, By encouraging the people to learn, grow, and become familiar with new skills, you are rewarding your company with the cheapest way to achieve team greatness.

Fund Services, not Projects

Usually companies work in a way where the Development and Test teams work on one project until they complete it and spend the funding, then on another, and on another, and so on.

Unfortunately, this is not only unproductive but also not motivating at all. This way your team cannot really see what are the long-term outcomes of their decisions.

Instead of doing the traditional funding, why not provide your teams with the ability to have the funds to perform their strategies and make the calls whenever they need to.

Another thing you should do is not to measure your projects the traditional way and check if it was completed within the given deadline, but appreciate the made achievements like profit, or other outcomes.

Keeping it Small with the Conway's Law

As the businesses expand and companies grow bigger, the main problem that appears is the inability for the people who work together to maintain a good communication. Think about it. It is kind of hard to maintain the same effectiveness of collaboration if some of you are shipped on a different floor, or another building.

Designing your team with the Conway's law means keeping the team sizes small in order to maintain the same communication patterns.

If you think that this is impossible, maybe you should consider taking the Amazon's advice and use their famous two pizza rule. What is the two pizza rule? The two pizza rule is the Amazon's rule of a thumb for keeping their teams small. If there is a team that cannot be fed with two pizzas, that means that it is too big.

Your teams should include 5-10 people on average.

Choosing to limit the size of the number of people in your teams will:

- Ensure that your teams have a great understanding of what they are working on. The larger the team, the poorer the communication and understanding.

- Limit the system's evolving rate. When you limit the size of your teams you also limit the growth rate of the system that they are working on.

- Enable autonomy. The smaller the team the more independently the people will work, which can be a great motivation-booster and produce a better outcome.

- Provide leadership experience. Using the two-pizza method you are providing every team member with the opportunity to express themselves which can help them grow professionally.

Their Majesties, the Three Ways

Despite the fact that DevOps was created in 2008, for most people, it is still hard to cut through the giant hype that has cloaked DevOps, and get to its core. What exactly is DevOps? If it was a software, a piece of hardware, or a single principle for that matter, it would be a lot easier to explain and understand DevOps. And although we have already said how this new methodology is more of a mindset and culture, the best way to grasp the true meaning of DevOps is to know what is made of.

Everything has to be built upon something. And to truly understand something, you have to know how it works. In order for you to be able to successfully adopt DevOps and spread this culture among the other employees, you need to be fully aware of its structure first.

The core underpinning DevOps, the basic principles that all other DevOps values are based on, is called *The Three Ways*. The three ways (developed by Gene Kim, the author of "The Phoenix Project", a great read by the way) are the three basic principles that represent the base of DevOps. They represent the philosophy that is guilty of framing the DevOps practices and processes. To truly understand DevOps, you have to get a good handle of *the three ways* first.

The First Way: System Thinking and Flow

DevOps thinks in systems, in set of practices and processes that work together in order to achieve a common goal. For DevOps, the system is the whole business, not a certain silo or some department, but the combination of all the smaller parts that contribute to bringing value to customers.

This *system thinking* is focused on the smooth collaboration and the flow of work. The first way represents just that. The flow between the business areas that are responsible for delivering the work to the customers.

In the world of technology, this flow starts in the Development department, where the work requirements are built, and then proceeds to the IT department, where the work is delivered to customers.

The focus of the first way is to make sure that the work flows smoothly. That can be done by increasing the quality of the provided service and decreasing the time needed for production and making changes of the work. The flow can only be increased if the work is visible, the batch sizes are reduced, the number of handoffs is reduced, and the waste in the value stream is eliminated.

Making the Work Visible

The downside of the technology value stream is that it is invisible. Think about it. The manufacturing value stream is visible because it has to be physically moved from one place to another. This makes the whole process a lot easier since the flaws can be easily detected. The technology value stream, on the other hand, is not that easy to be inspected. Unlike the manufacturing, the technology value stream is not transferred physically, but virtually, with a single click of a button. This may be more convenient, but it can also easily lead to delivering incomplete work to customers.

In order for us to see what stalls the work and support better flow, we need to try and make it as more visible as possible. The best way to improve the work flow is to use visual work boards that will represent the work stages in columns, from left to right. You can do this on physical or electronic cards by using Kanban or sprint planning boards.

Limiting Multitasking

Multitasking is something that is very common in the technology world. While in manufacturing it is easy to control and organize the daily work, technology workers are known to have much more dynamic jobs. They get easily interrupted due to the fact that the work is mainly invisible, which only increases their work that is in progress.

Limiting the work in progress and multitasking is another way of increasing the flow. You can do it also by using a Kanban board. For example, you can set a rule that the board can only take three or four works that are in progress. No new work can be accepted if there is not a free spot on the board.

Reducing the Batch Size

Doing the work in small batch sizes is one of the most important factors that can lead to improving the flow of the value stream and increasing the quality of the work. Here is why. If you perform the work in large batch sizes, obviously, it will take you a lot more time to complete it. Now you may think that this may reduce some of the costs, but in fact, this can easily backfire. How? Just imagine what can happen if a problem is found. The batch will probably get cancelled, a lot of time will be lost, and the result will be – poor quality or unsatisfied customers.

When doing things in small batches, on the other hand, the work is performed in small steps. That way, when a problem occurs, only a single step has to be repeated. This will not affect the whole work, and it can get done in a timely manner.

Reducing the Handoffs Number

Have you ever played the telephone game? You know, the one where you have to whisper a word to a friend, who has to repeat it to someone else, who has to repeat it to a fourth person, and so on. The game is fun because as soon as people start repeating the word, it begins to lose its context, and in most cases, the last person who has to say it out loud, says something entirely different.

But as much as you may enjoy this as a kid, you probably wouldn't like to play this game while working. Unfortunately, for technology workers, this is common. A long, technology deployment requires tons of codes and operations to be completed, which involves many different departments. In order for It to get completed, the work bounces from one team to another, and so on. But just like in the telephone game, when there are that many handoffs, the work begins to lose its context and the final outcome is often not as great as expected.

To increase the value stream flow, it is important that the number of handoffs is reduced. Although it may seem complicated, this can be easily done if the departments are organized to be less dependent on others by delivering a portion of the work to customers themselves.

Eliminating Waste

When we say waste, we mean anything that can affect the quality of the work and that can cause delay and inconveniences for our customers. The goal is to first make the wastes visible, and then do what's necessary to eliminate them in order to improve the flow of the work and achieve the final goal faster. Here are some good examples of wastes that your company may be dealing with:

- Partially done work. All of the work that is waiting in queue and still hasn't been completed is considered to be partially done. Do your best to eliminate these wastes as soon as possible, because they really slow done the entire work flow.

- Extra processes. All of the work that is additional and that does not bring a significant value to the final outcome, is considered to be an extra process. Whether it is not used documentations or invaluable reviews, do your best to eliminate what it's not important.

- Task switching. Assigning multiple projects to a single worker is not beneficial. Task switching can only add extra effort and increase the time necessary for deployment.

- Defects. Incorrect work and materials that are not clear create waste that needs to be eliminated. Make sure to get rid of the defects as they appear, and avoid putting extra effort to the flow of work.

The Second Way: Feedback Loops

The second way is the opposite of the first one. If the first way was all about increasing the flow of work from left to right, from development through IT to customers, the second way represent the feedback from the customers to the developers. The second way is focused on the principles that enable the feedback at each of the stages of the value stream.

What this means is that this part of DevOps is considered with creating left-to-right feedback loops. Its main goal is to make the feedback loops shorter and to respond to customers quickly in order to make early corrections when necessary and improve the customer's satisfaction.

This does not only give you the opportunity to satisfy their needs in time, but making fast and frequent changes also enables you to fix problems when they are still small and cheaper, which significantly reduces the costs.

See the Problems as They Occur

One of your main goals should be testing assumptions quickly. That means that you should increase the flow of information between the effect and the cause of the problem, and you should do it soon and fast. The more assumptions you test, the sooner you can fix the problems.

This can be done only when there are feedback loops created. In the technology world, however, this is not always the case. When there is a waterfall software project used, for example, the outcome is very poor because there is no fast feedback. The work is usually developed for a long time, and the feedback is received only after the testing phase, or in some cases, after delivering the work.

Instead of doing these old-fashioned mistakes, the second way of DevOps is focused on seeing the problems on time. That means that there should be more test processes while developing the work in order to detect the problems early, and fix them on time.

Swarming and Fixing the Problems

Detecting the problems as they occur is crucial, but obviously, not enough. After seeing the problem you will need to swarm it instantly, not wait for the right time to fix it. Swarming immediately is important because:

- It avoids the transportation of the problem to the next stage, when, chances us, there will be need for a higher effort and cost to fix it.

- It prevents us from starting new work while dragging the problem, which avoids the occurrence of new errors.

- It avoids the repetition of the same problem. If the problem is addressed immediately, that will probably prevent the team from making the same mistake in the following operation.

Pushing the Quality to Where the Work is Performed

The point is that you need to have everyone who is in your value stream working on detecting and fixing errors in their control area. That is the only way for pushing the work towards the source.

The best way to achieve that is to avoid:

- Assigning a team to complete work when it can easily be automatically done by the downstream team.

- Requiring busy people to make forced approvals that may not be so thoroughly considered.

- Asking for approval on a large batch of work at once, and then waiting for the responses.

Optimizing for the Next Customer

The customers are, obviously, the most important link in the chain, however, not to all departments. Although everyone in the company should work toward delivering satisfactory work to the customers, some departments should be more concerned with what the downstream work center (the next link in the chain) needs.

Lean methodology recognizes two types of customers, external and internal. The external customer is the one that pays to receive the desired service, and the internal customer is the department that is on the next step downstream. That means that the internal customer is the department that another department must forward the work to.

According to DevOps, the most important customer is the one that the team needs to send the work to. Each team must optimize their work for whoever is next on the line of receiving it. That way the internal feedback will be better, and the time for satisfying the external customer will be decreased.

The Third Way: Experimentation and Learning

If the first way was about improving the work flow from left to right, the second about receiving fast feedback from right to left, the third way represents making a culture that fosters experimentation and continual learning.

This principle of DevOps is concerned with creating a culture within the company where the workers will acknowledge that they can only master through practice and repetition. That basically means that every worker must learn that they are learners who must take risk on a daily basis. Whatever the outcome of the work, whether a success or a failure, it must be accepted and used as a lesson.

Experimenting and taking risk is the main focus of the third way, because it enables the workers to go deeper and strive for achieving even better results. The continual learning is also crucial because it is what helps them retreat when they have gone too far and help them learn what should and shouldn't be done.

Enabling Organizational Learning

There are three types of organizations:

a) Pathological organizations – characterized with threats and fear. The failure here is hidden, and people usually withhold information and do what it takes in order to present themselves in a good light.

b) Bureaucratic organizations – characterized by following processes and ruled. The failure here is judged and punished.

c) Generative organizations – characterized by searching for information that will help the entire organization to achieve its goal. The responsibilities here are shared, and the failure is usually reflected and causes inquiry.

In order to create a safe environment and a healthy system of work, the technology value stream must be established upon a generative culture. When a failure happens, instead of pointing fingers and looking for a way to punish the responsible team, the entire company should join forces in order to find a way to fix and redesign the system so that mistake can never happen again. That is how you can enable organizational learning.

You may want to take the advice from one engineer at Etsy and remove the blame and fear, in order to enable honesty which will lead to prevention.

Improving the Daily Work

We are used to avoiding solving our problems, and so we drag them along with the new ones that occur, just to find ourselves even more stressed out an unable to function properly. The same thing goes for the technology value stream. When we put fixing our problems on hold, new ones arise, the debt starts accumulating, and all that we can do is do workarounds without any productive cycles.

In order for you to improve your daily work you must first get rid of all the things that slow you down and prevent you from being as productive as you are needed to be. That is why reserving interval cycles important. What do I mean by that? What I am trying to say is that you should schedule some time to organize yourselves on fixing the current problems. Everyone should find and get rid of some defect in their area, and this should be done on regular basis. That way, when the system is much safer, the productivity and daily work get improved significantly.

Transforming Local to Global Success

When a team discovers or achieves something locally, it must be shared with the entire company. No, not verbally or for braging purposes, but through a mechanism that will help the others learn that knowledge through practice. That means that whenever a certain team delivers expertise, the company should turn it into codified knowledge. That way the rest of the company can achieve that expertise through practice, which will transform their local success globally.

Becoming Resilient

Like I said, doing experiments can help your company grow stronger. Checking the level of vulnerability and injecting resilience will help you understand just how capable you are, which will then enable you to find ways to support or improve your performance.

Introducing some stress and tension is inevitable for creating a healthy and strong work environment. I know it may not sound like it, but that is actually the only way you can increase your productivity.

Just remember those fire drills you did at school. Those weren't meant to scare you but to make you prepared for a safe evacuation in case of an actual fire. You may learn, perhaps, that you are too slow and need to work on your condition if you want to get out of a burning building alive. Well, just like those fire drills, your company also needs some experiments in order to teach you just how productive you are, and what needs to be improved.

This can be easily done by simply scheduling a *test day* from time to time. This test day should be filled with failure exercises, when you will, for instance, turn some work center off, just to see how resilient you will be in case of an emergency. One of the most famous DevOps companies, Netflix, has a great resilience test called

Chaos Monkey, when all of their servers and processes are killed in order to see if the company is as strong as they want it to be.

Forcing Leaders and Workers to Learn Together

In many companies, leaders are the ones that pull the strings. But just because they should set the objectives, that does not mean that leaders necessarily make the right decisions. Leaders are not there to create success; they are in charge of setting conditions that will allow the workers to bring the success through their daily work.

Leaders and workers must work and learn together in order for the company to be productive. Why? Simply because they need each other. The leaders do not have the knowledge it takes for performing the actual work, and the workers are not authorized or competent to make changes outside of their work area.

Together, they must create shorter and iterative goals that will contribute to global improvement.

Integrating Security

Security is an enormous part of the DevOps culture. But here, we will not we will not add security at the end, after the work is done. The security should be a part of everyone's daily job, and so, DevOps integrates daily security controls into Development and Operations, to ensure a safe and productive working environment.

Making Development Iteration Demonstrations Secure

DevOps is not about doing things the traditional, but the safe way. Therefore, one of its very important steps to productivity is not engaging Infosec at the end like usual. Instead, DevOps encourages inviting Infosec to the demonstrations, after each development interval. This does not only helps everyone understand the team goals better, but it also provides early feedback, which is extremely important.

Engaging Infosec in the early stages (even if they are only invited to observe) will help them gain a better grasp of the context and eventually make good risk-based decisions.

Integrating Security into Tracking Systems and Post Mortems

Traditionally, Infosec stored all of the security vulnerabilities in a GRC tool (Government, Risk, Compliance). Here, we want to put them in the systems used by Dev and Ops. It is important that we place all of those securities issues that are open in the work tracking system that is used by the Development and Operations. That way everything can be visible as well as well-ordered.

Besides that, it is also important for a Post-Mortem to be conducted after each security issue. This is great for teaching the security knowledge to the team of engineers, and make them easily learn how to prevent the same issues from happening in the future.

Integrating Security Controls Into Shared Services and Shared Source Code Repositories

Shared source code repositories are a great way to provide people with the opportunity to discover and use the company's knowledge for code, deployment pipeline, toolchains, and security. Since DevOps uses version control for all of the things that the company builds or even supports, it is more than a wise choice for that to be the place for all of the security artifacts. This way everyone can be aware of the new changes that may be made.

Making Sure the Application is Secure

To make sure the application is secure, obviously, you need to perform security tests. There are two types of these tests – happy path and sad path. Hapy path tests are developing tests that are focused on finding no error. On the other hand, sad path tests are focused on the things (especially security-related) that could go wrong.

And since performing the tests manually is almost impossible to execute, the best way is to make these tests a part of an automated unit that will be run continuously. Here is what it is important to include:

- Static Analysis – This is a type of test that is best performed during a non-runtime, and it is in charge of inspecting program code in order to find coding flaws or some malicious code. Code Climate and Brakeman are some great tools.

- Dynamic Analysis – This test is performed while the program is running, and it is in charge of monitoring response time, memory, and other performance-related issues. It is ideal to perform this test while the automated functional testing is active. Owasp Zap is one great tool that can be used for that purpose.

- Dependency Scanning - is a type of test that is performed inside the deployment pipeline, during build time, and it scans for potential malicious binaries. A great example is Owasp Dependency Check, as well as Maven for Java.

- Code Integrating and Signing – Every developer has to have their PGP key, an ideally, it should be created with something like *keybase.io*. The commits to the version control, as well as all of the process created by CI, should be signed.

Integrating Information Security Into Production Telemetry

The internal security controls have proven to be quite ineffective when it comes to detecting breaches in a short amount of time. This is caused either because there are blind spots in our monitoring, or because no one includes examining the telemetry into their daily work.

If you want to solve this issue, then you should consider integrating security telemetry into the tools that are used by QA, Development, and Operations. This give everyone in the pipeline the chance to see how the application is performing in a threat environment where attackers are seeking to gain unauthorized data and commit fraud.

Once you illuminate how the system can actually be attacked, you can reinforce the fact that security should be everyone's concern and that everyone should be involved with designing proper countermeasures.

Integrating Security Into the Development Pipeline

The main goal here is to make sure that both Development and Operations will be notified quickly after they make a certain change that is considered to be insecure. That way they can adopt detecting and fixing security issues as a normal part of the daily work which will contribute to an error-free, secure future.

It is ideal that the security tests are run in the deployment pipeline with some other tools for static code analysis. A great tool for this tests is Gauntlt, which is designed to run tests on the application, environment, etc. automatically. This amazing tool also places all of these tests in the Gherkin syntax which is what developers usually use.

This is by far the fastest way to provide feedback and allow Development and Operations to do their job the safest way possible.

Protecting the Deployment Pipe

The best way possible where you can find the malicious code is in the unit tests. Why? Because no one ever bothers to look at them and because every time that someone commits code to the repo, the unit tests are run. That being said, the only goof way in which you can protect the integrity of the environments and applications, a mitigation of the attack vectors on the deployment pipelines is required.

To protect the integration, deployment pipeline, and the continuous build, using these strategies is your best shield:

- Hardening the integration servers and the continuous build, and making sure that they can be reproduced in a timely manner, is the only way to prevent them from getting compromised.

- Reviewing the changes in the version control that are introduced by pair programming or code reviewing, to make sure that the continuous integration servers will not run uncontrolled codes.

- Instrumenting the repository to find out when the test code holds suspicious API calls.

- Making sure that every CI process runs on a VM or its isolated container.

- Making sure that the version control credentials that are used by the CI are in a read-only version.

Conclusion

In this uncertain technology era, where transformation is something that happens with a lightning speed, where security gets easily violated and every technological company struggles with ensuring agility, DevOps is something that brings reassurance.

I hope that this book was able to help you understand the principles and values of DevOps and why this modern culture can be your company's biggest asset.

Now that you know how this methodology works, the next step is to start spreading its ideals and force your company to think DevOps.

www.ingramcontent.com/pod-product-compliance
Lightning Source LLC
Chambersburg PA
CBHW051247170526
45165CB00004B/1611